RACHE

Magnificent Power

recognizing God is bigger than anything

BIBLE READING PLAN & JOURNAL

MAGNIFICENT POWER
Bible Reading Plan and Journal
PUBLISHED BY RACHEL WOJO
Copyright © 2017 by Rachel Wojnarowski

Visit **www.rachelwojo.com/shop**

Requests for information should be addressed to rachel@rachelwojo.com

Trade Paperback

ISBN-13: 978-0692940600 (Rachel Wojo LLC)

ISBN-10: 069294060X

Cover design by Rachel Wojnarowski

Photo credit: Bigstock.com

Library of Congress Cataloging-in-Publication Data

Printed in the United States of America
2017—First Edition--1001

Table of Contents

Intro: Magnificent Power

A Personal Note from Rachel

Day 1   Job 26:1-6

Day 2   Job 26:7-14

Day 3   Psalm 147:1-9

Day 4   Psalm 147:10-20

Day 5   Job 37:1-5

Day 6   Job 37:6-13

Day 7   Job 37:14-24

Day 8   Psalm 62:9-12

Day 9   Jeremiah 10:10-16

Day 10   Jeremiah 32:17-27

Day 11   Revelations 4:8-11

Day 12   Romans 1:16-25

Day 13   1 Corinthians 1:17-24

Day 14   1 Corinthians 1: 25-31

Day 15   Ephesians 1:18-23

Table of Contents

Day 16   1 Timothy 6:12-19

Day 17   Psalm 71:9-16

Day 18   Psalm 71:17-24

Day 19   2 Corinthians 13:1-5

Day 20   Matthew 19:16-26

Day 21   Psalm 66:1-9

Day 22   Psalm 66:10-20

Day 23   Jeremiah 10:10-16

Day 24   Isaiah 45:1-7

Day 25   Isaiah 45:8-14

Day 26   Isaiah 45:15-19

Day 27   Isaiah 45:20-25

Day 28   Ephesians 3:7-13

Day 29   Ephesians 3:14-21

Day 30   1 Corinthians 2:1-8

Day 31   1 Corinthians 2:9-16

A Personal Note from Rachel

Dear Friend,

Thank you for beginning this wonderful journaling experience through God's Word. My goal through Bible reading is to draw closer to Jesus, and I want that for you too!

Through reading daily Bible passages, praying, and listening to God, we're going to nurture and grow our relationship with him. This Bible reading plan and journal is specifically focused on recognizing God's magnificent power: his omnipotence.

The journey of life can feel like a rollercoaster, can't it? Just when it seems we're learning to rely on the Lord, we face another bump in the road or a mountain to climb over. This Bible reading plan will help us recognize the mighty power of our awesome God!

I'm thrilled to have you joining me! I pray you find the journaling section to be the perfect space for your individual needs.

Rachel

Remembering God is Bigger than Anything

Welcome to the Magnificent Power Bible Reading Plan and Journal. I'm so excited to begin this journey with you! For the next thirty-one days, we are going to dig into God's word and grow closer to Him. Together we'll decide to remove our eyes from the seemingly uphill battle of life and direct our attention to the incredible power and authority of God.

> I can take comfort in the fact that God's plan is always bigger and better than mine.
> --*One More Step*

Are you ready to transform your perspective from the smallness of this world to the largeness of who God is? You can share what you are learning on social media by using the hashtags #magnificentpower #godisbiggerjournal and #biblereadingplan. Or you can just keep it between you and God.

4 Simple Steps
to growing in faith

step 1:

Pray: Spend some time with God in prayer. Prayer is simply having a conversation with him.

step 2:

Read the Bible passage for the day one time slowly, soaking in each phrase. Read again if time allows.

step 3:

Answer the daily question.

step 4:

Complete the journaling section.

The Magnificent Power of God

Blessed are you, O Lord, the God of Israel our father, forever and ever. Yours, O Lord, is the greatness and the power and the glory and the victory and the majesty, for all that is in the heavens and in the earth is yours. Yours is the kingdom, O Lord, and you are exalted as head above all. Both riches and honor come from you, and you rule over all. In your hand are power and might, and in your hand, it is to make great and to give strength to all. And now we thank you, our God, and praise your glorious name. 1 Chronicles 29:10-13

In the Scripture before the passage above, David announced that Solomon would now be king and the work of building a temple for the Lord would be under his direction. He tells the people that he has made financial provisions for the building, but he asks the people of Israel to consecrate their hearts to this project and give whatever they can. After collecting all the offerings, the people rejoiced and David prayed this prayer. David knew that no matter the budget, God is the One who would provide all power and strength for the task ahead.

GOD IS BIGGER THAN...

Go ahead. Fill in the blank with whatever it is that you need to remember.

Is it an upcoming schedule change? Oh yes, he is bigger. How about a recent family crisis? He has every member in the palm of his hand. A new job? He's got it all under control.

How can we fill our minds with the faith to remember that God is sovereign over every human being and his power extends from the vast universe to the tiniest molecule? By saturating our hearts and minds with his word! Let's begin!

Give God glory.
How can I see God's
power in the details
of my life right now?

God gives me
breath when I have
none.

_____
_____
_____
_____
_____
_____
_____
_____

Today I have noticed or will strive to notice God's mighty
power at work in one or more of these areas:
(Circle your focus.)
Prayers Answered
Needs Provided
Promises Remembered
Strength Given
Abilities Issued
Talents Preserved
Opportunities Offered
Situations Controlled
Blessings Bestowed

From today's passage, write the words or phrases that describe God's power in random order below. You can then use this exercise as a word base for meditation, prayer and praise.

Pen A Prayer

Lord, I pray for my children and grandchildren, have mercy on them Lord, help them to know you and trust you. Preserve the marriages of my children and give them joy. Help them to see you and be thankful for all you have done for them. I ask humbly Lord. Amen

Power

I want to examine less why's and embrace more of His ways.

Take it to the Lord.
What is blocking my ability to see that God is in total control?

_____
_____
_____
_____
_____
_____
_____
_____

Today I have noticed or will strive to notice God's mighty power at work in one or more of these areas:

(Circle your focus.)

Prayers Answered

Needs Provided

Promises Remembered

Strength Given

Abilities Issued

Talents Preserved

Opportunities Offered

Situations Controlled

Blessings Bestowed

From today's passage, write the words or phrases that describe God's power in random order below. You can then use this exercise as a word base for meditation, prayer and praise.

Pen A Prayer

_____

_____

_____

_____

_____

_____

_____

_____

Healed

Give God glory.
How can I see God's
power in the details
of my life right now?

The One who
tends to the sea is
tender to me.

_____
_____
_____
_____
_____
_____
_____
_____
_____

Today I have noticed or will strive to notice God's mighty
power at work in one or more of these areas:

(Circle your focus.)

Prayers Answered

Needs Provided

Promises Remembered

Strength Given

Abilities Issued

Talents Preserved

Opportunities Offered

Situations Controlled

Blessings Bestowed

From today's passage, write the words or phrases that describe God's power in random order below. You can then use this exercise as a word base for meditation, prayer and praise.

Pen A Prayer

_____

_____

_____

_____

_____

_____

_____

_____

I sing the mighty
power of God,
that made the
mountains rise,
That spread the
flowing seas abroad,
and built the lofty
skies.
I sing the wisdom
that ordained the sun
to rule the day;
The moon shines full
at His command, and
all the stars obey.
Isaac Watts

Strength

May I realize my limitations and recognize His unlimited power.

Take it to the Lord.
What is blocking my ability to see that God is in total control?

_____
_____
_____
_____
_____
_____
_____
_____

Today I have noticed or will strive to notice God's mighty power at work in one or more of these areas:

(Circle your focus.)

Prayers Answered

Needs Provided

Promises Remembered

Strength Given

Abilities Issued

Talents Preserved

Opportunities Offered

Situations Controlled

Blessings Bestowed

From today's passage, write the words or phrases that describe God's power in random order below. You can then use this exercise as a word base for meditation, prayer and praise.

Pen A Prayer

_____

_____

_____

_____

_____

_____

_____

_____

Understand

God does great things that I cannot comprehend.

Give God glory.
How can I see God's power in the details of my life right now?

_____
_____
_____
_____
_____
_____
_____
_____

Today I have noticed or will strive notice God's mighty power at work in one or more of these areas:

(Circle your focus.)

Prayers Answered

Needs Provided

Promises Remembered

Strength Given

Abilities Issued

Talents Preserved

Opportunities Offered

Situations Controlled

Blessings Bestowed

From today's passage, write the words or phrases that describe God's power in random order below. You can then use this exercise as a word base for meditation, prayer and praise.

Pen A Prayer

_____

_____

_____

_____

_____

_____

_____

_____

Love

God corrects me
and sustains me.

Take it to the Lord.
What is blocking my
ability to see that God
is in total control?

_____
_____
_____
_____
_____
_____
_____
_____

Today I have noticed or will strive to notice God's
mighty power at work in one or more of these areas:
(Circle your focus.)
Prayers Answered
Needs Provided
Promises Remembered
Strength Given
Abilities Issued
Talents Preserved
Opportunities Offered
Situations Controlled
Blessings Bestowed

From today's passage, write the words or phrases that describe God's power in random order below. You can then use this exercise as a word base for meditation, prayer and praise.

Pen A Prayer

_____

_____

_____

_____

_____

_____

_____

_____

Emptiness of
soul
can only be
replaced
by the
fullness of God.

—Rachel Wojo,
One More Step

Wondrous

Gods work in the
past reminds me
today that He is
bigger.

Give God glory.
How can I see God's
power in the details
of my life right now?

_____
_____
_____
_____
_____
_____
_____
_____
_____

Today I have noticed or will strive to notice God's
mighty power at work in one or more of these areas:
(Circle your focus.)
Prayers Answered
Needs Provided
Promises Remembered
Strength Given
Abilities Issued
Talents Preserved
Opportunities Offered
Situations Controlled
Blessings Bestowed

From today's passage, write the words or phrases that describe God's power in random order below. You can then use this exercise as a word base for meditation, prayer and praise.

Pen A Prayer

_____

_____

_____

_____

_____

_____

_____

_____

Power

Do I believe that
God holds the
power and love in
my life?

Take it to the Lord.
What is blocking my
ability to see that God
is in total control?

_____
_____
_____
_____
_____
_____
_____
_____

Today I have noticed or will strive to notice God's mighty
power at work in one or more of these areas:
(Circle your focus.)
Prayers Answered
Needs Provided
Promises Remembered
Strength Given
Abilities Issued
Talents Preserved
Opportunities Offered
Situations Controlled
Blessings Bestowed

From today's passage, write the words or phrases that describe God's power in random order below. You can then use this exercise as a word base for meditation, prayer and praise.

Pen A Prayer

_____

_____

_____

_____

_____

_____

_____

_____

Wisdom

God holds all power, wisdom and understanding.

Give God glory.
How can I see God's power in the details of my life right now?

_____

_____

_____

_____

_____

_____

_____

_____

Today I have noticed or will strive to notice God's mighty power at work in one or more of these areas:

(Circle your focus.)

Prayers Answered

Needs Provided

Promises Remembered

Strength Given

Abilities Issued

Talents Preserved

Opportunities Offered

Situations Controlled

Blessings Bestowed

From today's passage, write the words or phrases that describe God's power in random order below. You can then use this exercise as a word base for meditation, prayer and praise.

Pen A Prayer

_____

_____

_____

_____

_____

_____

_____

_____

It is he who made the earth
by his power,
who established the world
by his wisdom,
and by his understanding
stretched out the heavens.
Jeremiah 10:12

Nothing

Nothing is too hard for God.

Take it to the Lord.
What is blocking my
ability to see that God
is in total control?

_____
_____
_____
_____
_____
_____
_____
_____

Today I have noticed or will strive to notice God's mighty
power at work in one or more of these areas:
(Circle your focus.)

Prayers Answered

Needs Provided

Promises Remembered

Strength Given

Abilities Issued

Talents Preserved

Opportunities Offered

Situations Controlled

Blessings Bestowed

From today's passage, write the words or phrases that describe God's power in random order below. You can then use this exercise as a word base for meditation, prayer and praise.

Pen A Prayer

_____

_____

_____

_____

_____

_____

_____

_____

The God
who created
the universe
rules over it.

Worthy

My God created
all things and by
His will they
exist.

Give God glory.
How can I see God's
power in the details
of my life right now?

_____
_____
_____
_____
_____
_____
_____
_____
_____

Today I have noticed or will strive to notice God's mighty
power at work in one or more of these areas:
(Circle your focus.)
Prayers Answered
Needs Provided
Promises Remembered
Strength Given
Abilities Issued
Talents Preserved
Opportunities Offered
Situations Controlled
Blessings Bestowed

From today's passage, write the words or phrases that describe God's power in random order below. You can then use this exercise as a word base for meditation, prayer and praise.

Pen A Prayer

_____

_____

_____

_____

_____

_____

_____

_____

Eternal

Since creation, God has revealed himself through what He has made.

Take it to the Lord.
What is blocking my ability to see that God is in total control?

_____
_____
_____
_____
_____
_____
_____
_____

Today I have noticed or will strive to notice God's mighty power at work in one or more of these areas:
(Circle your focus.)
Prayers Answered
Needs Provided
Promises Remembered
Strength Given
Abilities Issued
Talents Preserved
Opportunities Offered
Situations Controlled
Blessings Bestowed

From today's passage, write the words or phrases that describe God's power in random order below. You can then use this exercise as a word base for meditation, prayer and praise.

Pen A Prayer

_____

_____

_____

_____

_____

_____

_____

_____

Nothing

I must remember how God has brought me from nothing.

Give God glory.
How can I see God's power in the details of my life right now?

_____
_____
_____
_____
_____
_____
_____
_____
_____

Today I have noticed or will strive to notice God's mighty power at work in one or more of these areas:
(Circle your focus.)
Prayers Answered
Needs Provided
Promises Remembered
Strength Given
Abilities Issued
Talents Preserved
Opportunities Offered
Situations Controlled
Blessings Bestowed

From today's passage, write the words or phrases that describe God's power in random order below. You can then use this exercise as a word base for meditation, prayer and praise.

Pen A Prayer

_____

_____

_____

_____

_____

_____

_____

_____

Let the one
who boasts
boast
in the Lord.
1 Corinthians 1:31

Foolishness

The foolishness of man cannot be compared to God's knowledge and power.

Take it to the Lord. What is blocking my ability to see that God is in total control?

_____
_____
_____
_____
_____
_____
_____
_____

Today I have noticed or will strive to notice God's mighty power at work in one or more of these areas:

(Circle your focus.)

Prayers Answered

Needs Provided

Promises Remembered

Strength Given

Abilities Issued

Talents Preserved

Opportunities Offered

Situations Controlled

Blessings Bestowed

From today's passage, write the words or phrases that describe God's power in random order below. You can then use this exercise as a word base for meditation, prayer and praise.

Pen A Prayer

_____

_____

_____

_____

_____

_____

_____

_____

Enlighten

Let me see with
the eyes of my
heart to know
that God is bigger.

Give God glory.
How can I see God's
power in the details
of my life right now?

_____
_____
_____
_____
_____
_____
_____
_____

Today I have noticed or will strive to notice God's
mighty power at work in one or more of these areas:
(Circle your focus.)

Prayers Answered
Needs Provided
Promises Remembered
Strength Given
Abilities Issued
Talents Preserved
Opportunities Offered
Situations Controlled
Blessings Bestowed

From today's passage, write the words or phrases that describe God's power in random order below. You can then use this exercise as a word base for meditation, prayer and praise.

Pen A Prayer

_____

_____

_____

_____

_____

_____

_____

_____

Sovereign

Take it to the Lord.
What is blocking my
ability to see that God
is in total control?

_____
_____
_____
_____
_____
_____
_____
_____
_____

God alone is
immortal.

Today I have noticed or will strive to notice God's
mighty power at work in one or more of these areas:

(Circle your focus.)

Prayers Answered

Needs Provided

Promises Remembered

Strength Given

Abilities Issued

Talents Preserved

Opportunities Offered

Situations Controlled

Blessings Bestowed

From today's passage, write the words or phrases that describe God's power in random order below. You can then use this exercise as a word base for meditation, prayer and praise.

Pen A Prayer

_____

_____

_____

_____

_____

_____

_____

Immortal, invisible,
God only wise,
In light inaccessible,
hid from our eyes,
Most blessed, most glorious,
the Ancient of Days,
Almighty, victorious,
Thy great name we praise.

— *Walter C. Smith*
Immortal, Invisible

Unlimited

Give God glory.
How can I see God's power in the details of my life right now?

God's greatness is beyond my understanding.

_____
_____
_____
_____
_____
_____
_____
_____

Today I have noticed or will strive to notice God's mighty power at work in one or more of these areas:

(Circle your focus.)

Prayers Answered
Needs Provided
Promises Remembered
Strength Given
Abilities Issued
Talents Preserved
Opportunities Offered
Situations Controlled
Blessings Bestowed

From today's passage, write the words or phrases that describe God's power in random order below. You can then use this exercise as a word base for meditation, prayer and praise.

Pen A Prayer

_____

_____

_____

_____

_____

_____

_____

_____

faithful

My God is
radically faithful.

Take it to the Lord.
What is blocking my
ability to see that God
is in total control?

_____
_____
_____
_____
_____
_____
_____
_____
_____

Today I have noticed or will strive to notice God's mighty
power at work in one or more of these areas:
(Circle your focus.)
Prayers Answered
Needs Provided
Promises Remembered
Strength Given
Abilities Issued
Talents Preserved
Opportunities Offered
Situations Controlled
Blessings Bestowed

From today's passage, write the words or phrases that describe God's power in random order below. You can then use this exercise as a word base for meditation, prayer and praise.

Pen A Prayer

_____

_____

_____

_____

_____

_____

_____

_____

Mantra

When I am
crucified in
weakness, I can live
by God's power.

Give God glory.
How can I see God's
power in the details
of my life right now?

_____
_____
_____
_____
_____
_____
_____
_____
_____

Today I have noticed or will strive to notice God's mighty
power at work in one or more of these areas:
(Circle your focus.)
Prayers Answered
Needs Provided
Promises Remembered
Strength Given
Abilities Issued
Talents Preserved
Opportunities Offered
Situations Controlled
Blessings Bestowed

From today's passage, write the words or phrases that describe God's power in random order below. You can then use this exercise as a word base for meditation, prayer and praise.

Pen A Prayer

All

With God,
all things
are possible.

Take it to the Lord.
What is blocking my
ability to see that God
is in total control?

_____

_____

_____

_____

_____

_____

_____

Today I have noticed or will strive to notice God's mighty
power at work in one or more of these areas:
(Circle your focus.)
Prayers Answered
Needs Provided
Promises Remembered
Strength Given
Abilities Issued
Talents Preserved
Opportunities Offered
Situations Controlled
Blessings Bestowed

From today's passage, write the words or phrases that describe God's power in random order below. You can then use this exercise as a word base for meditation, prayer and praise.

Pen A Prayer

_____

_____

_____

_____

_____

_____

_____

_____

Miracles

Give God glory.
How can I see God's
power in the details
of my life right now?

_____
_____
_____

What red sea in my
life needs crossed
right now?

_____
_____
_____
_____
_____
_____

Today I have noticed or will strive to notice God's
mighty power at work in one or more of these areas:
(Circle your focus.)
Prayers Answered
Needs Provided
Promises Remembered
Strength Given
Abilities Issued
Talents Preserved
Opportunities Offered
Situations Controlled
Blessings Bestowed

From today's passage, write the words or phrases that describe God's power in random order below. You can then use this exercise as a word base for meditation, prayer and praise.

Pen A Prayer

_____

_____

_____

_____

_____

_____

_____

_____

God invites us to look
beyond
the little we have
to the largeness
of what
He offers.

—*Rachel Wojo,*
One More Step

Restore

God keeps me
alive and does not
allow my feet to
slip.

Take it to the Lord.
What is blocking my
ability to see that God
is in total control?

_____
_____
_____
_____
_____
_____
_____
_____

Today I have noticed or will strive to notice God's mighty
power at work in one or more of these areas:
(Circle your focus.)
Prayers Answered
Needs Provided
Promises Remembered
Strength Given
Abilities Issued
Talents Preserved
Opportunities Offered
Situations Controlled
Blessings Bestowed

From today's passage, write the words or phrases that describe God's power in random order below. You can then use this exercise as a word base for meditation, prayer and praise.

Pen A Prayer

_____

_____

_____

_____

_____

_____

_____

_____

Established

The Lord has
formed all things.

Give God glory.
How can I see God's
power in the details
of my life right now?

_____
_____
_____
_____
_____
_____
_____
_____
_____

Today I have noticed or will strive to notice God's mighty
power at work in one or more of these areas:
(Circle your focus.)
Prayers Answered
Needs Provided
Promises Remembered
Strength Given
Abilities Issued
Talents Preserved
Opportunities Offered
Situations Controlled
Blessings Bestowed

From today's passage, write the words or phrases that describe God's power in random order below. You can then use this exercise as a word base for meditation, prayer and praise.

Pen A Prayer

_____

_____

_____

_____

_____

_____

_____

_____

When things seem
out of control,
God is always
in control.
-One More Step

Over All

Take it to the Lord.
What is blocking my
ability to see that God
is in total control?

There is no God
but my God.

_____

_____

_____

_____

_____

_____

_____

_____

_____

Today I have noticed or will strive to notice God's
mighty power at work in one or more of these areas:
(Circle your focus.)
Prayers Answered
Needs Provided
Promises Remembered
Strength Given
Abilities Issued
Talents Preserved
Opportunities Offered
Situations Controlled
Blessings Bestowed

From today's passage, write the words or phrases that describe God's power in random order below. You can then use this exercise as a word base for meditation, prayer and praise.

Pen A Prayer

_____

_____

_____

_____

_____

_____

_____

Source

Give God glory.
How can I see God's
power in the details
of my life right now?

Righteousness
and strength
come only from
God.

_____
_____
_____
_____
_____
_____
_____
_____
_____

Today I have noticed or will strive to notice God's mighty
power at work in one or more of these areas:
(Circle your focus.)
Prayers Answered
Needs Provided
Promises Remembered
Strength Given
Abilities Issued
Talents Preserved
Opportunities Offered
Situations Controlled
Blessings Bestowed

From today's passage, write the words or phrases that describe God's power in random order below. You can then use this exercise as a word base for meditation, prayer and praise.

Pen A Prayer

_____

_____

_____

_____

_____

_____

_____

_____

For thus says the Lord,
who created the heavens
(he is God!),
who formed the earth and made it
(he established it;
he did not create it empty,
he formed it to be inhabited!):
"I am the Lord, and there is no other.
Isaiah 45:18

Intimate

The God of the universe is intimately interested in His creation.

Take it to the Lord.
What is blocking my ability to see that God is in total control?

_____
_____
_____
_____
_____
_____
_____
_____

Today I have noticed or will strive to notice God's mighty power at work in one or more of these areas:

(Circle your focus.)

Prayers Answered

Needs Provided

Promises Remembered

Strength Given

Abilities Issued

Talents Preserved

Opportunities Offered

Situations Controlled

Blessings Bestowed

From today's passage, write the words or phrases that describe God's power in random order below. You can then use this exercise as a word base for meditation, prayer and praise.

Pen A Prayer

_____

_____

_____

_____

_____

_____

_____

_____

Fullness

God longs for my heart to experience wholeness through Him.

Give God glory.
How can I see God's power in the details of my life right now?

_____
_____
_____
_____
_____
_____
_____
_____
_____

Today I have noticed or will strive to notice God's mighty power at work in one or more of these areas:

(Circle your focus.)

Prayers Answered

Needs Provided

Promises Remembered

Strength Given

Abilities Issued

Talents Preserved

Opportunities Offered

Situations Controlled

Blessings Bestowed

From today's passage, write the words or phrases that describe God's power in random order below. You can then use this exercise as a word base for meditation, prayer and praise.

Pen A Prayer

_____

_____

_____

_____

_____

_____

_____

_____

Glory

Jesus, may we
keep our eyes on
you today.

Take it to the Lord.
What is blocking my
ability to see that God
is in total control?

_____
_____
_____
_____
_____
_____
_____

Today I have noticed or will strive to notice God's
mighty power at work in one or more of these areas:
(Circle your focus.)
Prayers Answered
Needs Provided
Promises Remembered
Strength Given
Abilities Issued
Talents Preserved
Opportunities Offered
Situations Controlled
Blessings Bestowed

From today's passage, write the words or phrases that describe God's power in random order below. You can then use this exercise as a word base for meditation, prayer and praise.

Pen A Prayer

_____

_____

_____

_____

_____

_____

_____

_____

Capacity

When I am rooted in love, I have the power to understand God's love is incomprehensible.

Give God glory.
How can I see God's power in the details of my life right now?

_____

_____

_____

_____

_____

_____

_____

_____

Today I have noticed or will strive to God's mighty power at work in one or more of these areas:

(Circle your focus.)

Prayers Answered

Needs Provided

Promises Remembered

Strength Given

Abilities Issued

Talents Preserved

Opportunities Offered

Situations Controlled

Blessings Bestowed

From today's passage, write the words or phrases that describe God's power in random order below. You can then use this exercise as a word base for meditation, prayer and praise.

Pen A Prayer

_____

_____

_____

_____

_____

_____

_____

_____

Wisdom

The only power
or strength I have
comes from God.

Take it to the Lord.
What is blocking my
ability to see that God
is in total control?

_____
_____
_____
_____
_____
_____
_____
_____

Today I have noticed or will strive to notice God's mighty
power at work in one or more of these areas:
(Circle your focus.)
Prayers Answered
Needs Provided
Promises Remembered
Strength Given
Abilities Issued
Talents Preserved
Opportunities Offered
Situations Controlled
Blessings Bestowed

From today's passage, write the words or phrases that describe God's power in random order below. You can then use this exercise as a word base for meditation, prayer and praise.

Pen A Prayer

_____

_____

_____

_____

_____

_____

_____

_____

Belief

Give God glory.
How can I see God's
power in the details
of my life right now?

_____
_____
_____
_____
_____
_____
_____
_____

Faith is not based
on my wisdom
but on God's
power.

Today I have noticed or will strive to God's mighty
power at work in one or more of these areas:

(Circle your focus.)

Prayers Answered

Needs Provided

Promises Remembered

Strength Given

Abilities Issued

Talents Preserved

Opportunities Offered

Situations Controlled

Blessings Bestowed

From today's passage, write the words or phrases that describe God's power in random order below. You can then use this exercise as a word base for meditation, prayer and praise.

Pen A Prayer

_____

_____

_____

_____

_____

_____

_____

_____

Put a Bow on It!

You did it! You read your Bible for 31 days in a row!

Throughout this month of Scripture reading, I've been reminded that God's power and authority excels beyond and above anyone else. I have so enjoyed the pointed thought that God truly is bigger than anything that comes my way.

I pray that as you've walked this 31-day path, you've enjoyed the journaling methods and each one has spurred you on to embrace the almighty power of God at work everywhere!

May you continue to experience the comfort of his sovereignty and omnipotence.

Thanks for joining me on this journey through the Bible. Discover more Bible reading plans & journals at rachelwojo.com/shop.

Additional Notes

About the Author

Rachel "Wojo" Wojnarowski is wife to Matt and mom to seven wonderful kids. Her greatest passion is inspiring others to welcome Jesus into their lives and enjoy the abundant life he offers.

As a sought-after blogger and writer, she sees thousands of readers visit her blog daily. Rachel leads community ladies' Bible studies in central Ohio and serves as an event planner and speaker. In her "free time" she crochets, knits, and sews handmade clothing. Okay, not really. She enjoys running and she's a tech geek at heart.

Reader, writer, speaker, and dreamer, Rachel can be found on her website at **www.RachelWojo.com**.

Free Bible Study Video Series

If you enjoyed this Bible reading plan & journal, then you'll love Rachel's free video Bible study to help you find strength for difficult seasons of life! **http://rachelwojo.com/free-bible-study-video-series-for-one-more-step/**

Feel like giving up?

Are you ready to quit? Give up? But deep down, you want to figure out how to keep on keeping on?

Like you, Rachel has faced experiences that crushed her dreams of the perfect life: a failed marriage, a daughter's heartbreaking diagnosis, and more. In this book, she transparently shares her pain and empathizes with yours, then points you to the path of God's Word, where you'll find hope to carry you forward. One More Step gives you permission to ache freely—and helps you believe that life won't always be this hard. No matter the circumstances you face, through these pages you'll learn to...

- persevere through out-of-control circumstances and gain a more intimate relationship with Jesus
- run to God's Word when discouragement strikes
- replace feelings of despair with truths of Scripture

If you enjoyed this Bible reading plan and journal, then you'll love:

RACHEL WOJO

Pure Joy

cultivating a
happy heart

BIBLE READING PLAN & JOURNAL

RACHEL WOJO

True Love

embracing the Father's affection

BIBLE READING PLAN & JOURNAL

RACHEL WOJO

Perfect Peace

planting my eyes on Jesus

BIBLE READING PLAN & JOURNAL

RACHEL WOJO

Confident Trust

believing God's plan is best

BIBLE READING PLAN & JOURNAL

RACHEL WOJO

Never Alone

remembering
God is with me

BIBLE READING PLAN & JOURNAL

RACHEL WOJO

Soul Secure

winning over worry
through God's Word

BIBLE READING PLAN & JOURNAL

RACHEL WOJO

Purposeful Pause

waiting on God's perfect timing

BIBLE READING PLAN & JOURNAL

RACHEL WOJO

Everything Beautiful

savoring God's seasonal elegance

BIBLE READING PLAN & JOURNAL

http://rachelwojo.com/shop

Made in the USA
San Bernardino, CA
23 June 2018